Here's what others are saying abo

MW00990938

How many times have I looked at each individual child wondered if I would ever truly understand how to best ... as a mother, a teacher and a mentor? The You Zoo is a phenomenally practical, creative and inductive tool that will give you a much needed lens into viewing how your child thinks, feels and experiences life. You will laugh, affirm, celebrate and gain life-changing insight along with your child as together you are handed the gift of perspective with clarity, sensitivity and compassion.

GHENA M. BURSON, M. A., Curriculum & Instruction
Homeschooling mother of eight

In a world where educators embrace diversity in relation to socio-economic status and ability level, The You Zoo provides educators with information that can reach across cultures and performance levels to allow teachers to engage the true essence of the child.

DR. LEANN SMITH
Principal at Albin Elementary—A Blue Ribbon School

Albin Elementary implemented The You Zoo program through a school-wide assessment engaging students, teachers and parents. We followed up with professional development for teachers and parents analyzing results and learning the program's tips to meet the needs of the diverse personalities of our students. The You Zoo allowed us to have a deeper understanding of the "emotional currency" of each child. Teachers gained insight into more effective differentiation and classroom management. The You Zoo is fascinating and purposeful for any educator or parent.

TRACY PETSCH
Milken Educator at Albin Elementary School—A Blue Ribbon School

I have found out not only a lot about myself as a teacher but also about how my students learn from me because of their different personalities. Learning the student's personalities will help guide my future instruction. This will in turn guide my students to the best of their abilities.

LORI TREVILLYAN
2nd grade teacher

The YouZoo

Cover and interior design by Cindy Kiple

ISBN: 978-0-9835481-0-2

Medley Press
3204 Road 139
Meriden, WY 82081
307.246.3348
www.MedleyPress.com

www.YouZooKids.com

Children's Personality Assessment

Designed for use with grades Pre K through Six

Jami Kirkbride, L.P.C.

Licensed Professional Counselor and
Certified Personality Trainer

&

Kathryn Robbins, C.L.C.

President, Personality Principles LLC™
and Certified Life Coach

Illustrations by
Hannah England

Jami's Dedication

To my husband Jeff, who keeps our zoo in order: thanks for all you do.

To my wonderful children:

T.K., you want to do what's right and are a great example.

C.K., you have taught me true strength and determination.

J.K., you refresh my days with laughter, hugs and teasing.

S.K., you color my life with fun, spunk and imagination.

J.T.K, you delight my soul with snuggles and smiles.

Baby K., we are so anxious to meet you.

To my parents:

You have given me a life with love and God—thanks for your support.

I love you all dearly!

• •

Kathryn's Dedication

To my husband Steve, whose insights, edits, and patience is deeply appreciated.

To my sons:

Eric, who taught me how to give acceptance "as is."

Ryan, who helped me understand the art of letting go.

Drew, your one line wit is truly funny and helps lighten the mood.

Brett, your diligence to doing it right has been a great comfort.

Garrett, your ability to take a stand and choose the right path

makes parenting so much easier.

To my Daughters-in-law:

Kelly, Katie, Abigail and Nicole, you have enriched our family

and have helped us get one step closer to becoming a tribe.

To my Granddaughter Jenna, This book was developed with you in mind.

To all of my family: I love you!

Special Thanks

To the Creator who fashioned us with love to be the unique and wonderfully made people that we are. To the men and women of science and religion who have uncovered the true nature of man and have shown us how DNA affects our personal development. To the scriptures which expose our weakness, but also inspire us to live a life worthy of praise by living in our strengths.

To our friends and family members who have supported us through this journey by reading, re-reading, and reading again all the versions of this book as it was being developed. Thank you for your edits, opinions, and praise. Without you, we would not have anyone to help us practice what we preach.

To Florence Littauer, who introduced us to "The Personalities." Thank you for your years of generous mentoring, training, and friendship.

To Hannah England and Cindy Kiple, who helped bring our ideas and cute little monkey friends to life. You are blessed with great talent.

To all the Certified Personality Trainers, coaches, educators and parents who use these materials. Without you, we would be lone voices singing a single note.

To all: a big THANK YOU!

Table of Contents

Congratulations on choosing THE YOU ZOO

THE YOU ZOO Children's Personality Assessment Profile is an excellent way to discover your child's strengths, struggles, and emotional needs. Your willingness to take the time and effort to do the assessment with your child shows that you care about your child's development.

We each have five children and we know first hand the challenge of raising our children "in the way they should go." At the core of each child, there is a natural tendency to act, react, learn, communicate, and function in a certain way. It's built right into the fabric of his/her DNA. When you understand the framework in which your child operates, you can develop strategies, disciplines, and a plan that will work best for his/her personality type.

By the time your child reaches adulthood there will be many factors that shape who he/she becomes, including personality, birth order, gender, childhood experiences, adult experiences, spiritual education, and moral code. All of these factors mix to make each person an individual - never to be duplicated. Identifying personality types does not mean that you are putting your child in a box. Instead, this information will allow you to see his/her inborn tendencies.

Understanding your child's personality is an important step in developing natural strengths and overcoming potential struggles. By understanding how your child is hardwired, you can help shape and train his/her character, saving you and your child years of frustration and misunderstanding. Accepting our children's unique personality traits has a trickledown effect. When we are secure with who they are, they become secure and able to understand and accept themselves better.

As you work through this assessment with your child and read about the different personality traits, you will learn about yourself in the process. You will begin to understand areas where you are similar to your child, as well as areas where you are quite different. These insights are keys to working more effectively with your child.

We feel privileged to partner with you as you explore your child's development through his/her natural personality. It is our hope and goal that this tool will enable and encourage you to help your child become all she/he can be.

May the journey you take with your child be happy, productive, and enjoyable.

Have fun, learn, and grow!

Jami
Jami Kirkbride, L.P.C., C.P.T.
Licensed Professional Counselor
Certified Personality Trainer

Kathryn
Kathryn Robbins C.P.T., C.L.C.
President, Personality Principles LLC
Certified Personality Trainer/Life Coach

PART ONE

• • • • • • • • • • • • • •

The You Zoo

Children's Personality Assessment™

How to Complete THE YOU ZOO
Children's Personality Assessment™

THE YOU ZOO Children's Personality Assessment is designed with adult interaction in mind. The intent of this personality assessment is to help parents and teachers peek inside the development of the child as she/he grows and matures.

HOW TO COMPLETE THE ASSESSMENT

• Preschool: As you read each short scenario in the story, have your child follow along. Listen for any comments she/he may make, as this will help you understand his/her selection. Read the choices a second time, providing an opportunity to hear all the options again. Have your child place a finger on the monkey that is most like her/himself. Let your child make his/her own choices. Put a circle around the monkey's name along the bottom of the page that corresponds to his/her choice.

• Early readers: Have your child read each scenario in the story to you and help with any unknown words. Encourage your child to read the choices through again. Let him/her put a circle around the monkey at the bottom of each page that corresponds with his/her choice. Again, observe and answer any questions that come up.

• Older Elementary: Your child should be able to complete the assessment without much assistance, but remember there is value in watching how and why she/he makes selections.

VERBAL DIRECTIONS:

• Some children may want to select the choice you want them to pick, but it is important to remind them that there is no right or wrong answer. They should pick the monkey that they think is acting or thinking most like they would.

• Some children will want to just follow the pictures and skip reading the words, but the reason for the monkeys' behavior is important, so remind them to pay close attention to the words and reasons as well as the pictures.

USING THE SCORE SHEET:

• The score sheet is on page 43. Additional score sheets are included at the back of the book.

WRAPPING IT UP:

• At the end of the assessment, go back and review the individual responses. Ask your child about his/her particular answers and why she/he chose them. Make sure you do this carefully so the child doesn't feel like she/he did it wrong. This will help you understand the selections. The reasons your child offers may give additional information in identifying his/her personality type more accurately.

Monkey see, monkey do. Who are you?

Welcome to the famous You Zoo! This is the best zoo in the world, and the only one of its kind! Many interesting things go on around here. These animals talk, think, and have fun. But today, we are going straight for the monkey cage, home of the most exciting group of monkeys you will ever see. Sunny, Champ, Max, and Pal are smart monkeys and they have something to show you about yourself.

Even though these four monkeys all live together and do some things the same way, they are actually very different. They are unique and special just the way you are. Follow the story of the monkeys. In each situation decide which monkey is most like you. Which little monkey do you think you would be?

Monkey Tale 1

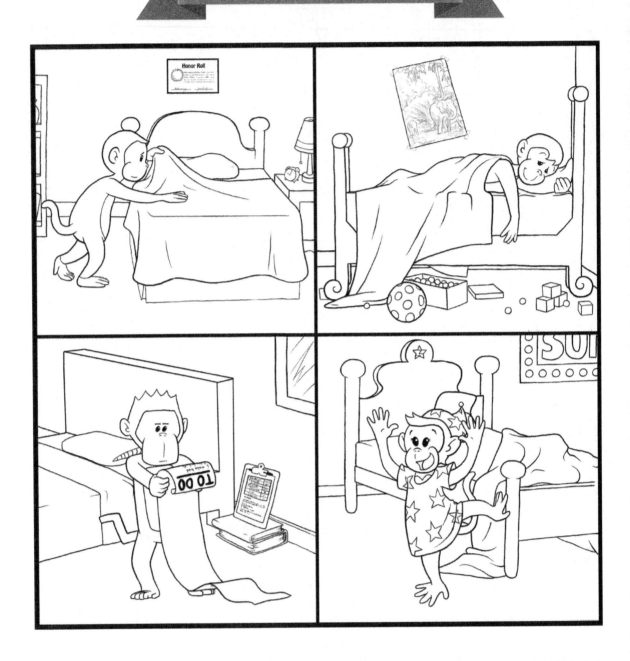

Good Morning or Not

The sun is rising at the You Zoo. The elephants trumpet the wake up call. The lions roar in the distance, and the birds sing their morning song. But they are not the only animals getting up. The four little monkeys are starting their day too.

Max does the same routine every morning. Doing things the right way really matters.

Pal wakes up slowly. Even without a routine, most mornings are happy times.

Champ wakes up with a plan and thinks everyone else should have one too.

Sunny either wakes up the happiest monkey in the whole wide world or the grumpiest of all the monkeys.

Circle the monkey most like you

| Max | Pal | Champ | Sunny |

Breakfast of "Chimpions"

Everyone is up and dressed, hair is combed, and beds are made. The monkeys are now ready for breakfast.

Champ likes to eat quickly. There is a plan and things to get done.

Sunny talks a lot and forgets to eat. A good story is part of every meal!

Max has a favorite spoon and bowl and is bothered when different foods touch.

Pal is pickier about what to eat. "I don't like trying new foods."

Circle the monkey most like you

| Champ | Sunny | Max | Pal |

Off to Work We Go

All of the monkeys have a chore in order to keep their space clean. They help sweep, do dishes, empty the trash, and pick up their toys.

Sunny likes to have fun while working, but forgets what is supposed to get done.

Champ is a good worker but doesn't really like to be told what to do.

Max likes it done the proper way and will spend a long time getting it right.

Pal can become overwhelmed if the job is too big or if there is too much to do.

Monkey Tale 4

Tricky Monkeys

The zookeeper likes to teach the monkeys new and amazing tricks, because they love to perform for the people. They know that is what makes them the zoo favorites.

Pal likes the easy tricks and wouldn't mind just doing the old ones.

Sunny loves the new tricks, especially if they are funny and make people laugh.

Champ likes the big tough tricks. This kind of challenge is exciting.

Max likes learning new tricks when alone. Others can see them after lots of practice so they are perfect.

Circle the monkey most like you

| Pal | Sunny | Champ | Max |

Getting the Show on the Road

The monkeys are so pleased with their new tricks they decide to make a movie. Each monkey will have a task.

Max is a good planner and will write the script. It's very important to get it just right.

Champ, of course, likes to be in charge and direct the show.

Sunny will be the shining star of the movie. Making others laugh is the best part!

Pal will do whatever others ask. That's what makes things run smoothly.

Circle the monkey most like you

| Max | Champ | Sunny | Pal |

Monkey Tale 6

It's All About the Costume

Once everyone decided what role they would play, they asked the zookeeper for their box of costumes. Each monkey eagerly dug through the box to find just the right costume.

Champ found one right away. A police hat would be a good choice for someone in charge.

Max thought carefully but decided the top hat would look neat, tidy, and smart.

Pal had a hard time deciding what to pick, but finally settled on being the cat.

Sunny was thrilled to find the superstar costume and couldn't wait to put it on.

Circle the monkey most like you

| Champ | Max | Pal | Sunny |

To Be – Or Not to Be

After Pal picked the cat, they all wanted to be a different animal. They thought about the other animals in the zoo. Oh, this was going to be fun!

Sunny jumped up and down. "Oh, I know, I know, I will be the butterfly…carefree and colorful!"

Champ thought the tiger was the best choice. Tigers are powerful and big.

Max took time deciding what animal was right – maybe the owl would be right, because people say owls are wise and deep thinkers.

Pal liked being the cat, but an elephant would be a good choice too, because elephants take good care of their families.

Circle the monkey most like you

| Sunny | Champ | Max | Pal |

Monkey Tale 8

The Beat Goes On

The parts and costumes have been decided. The movie would not be complete without music. They all had ideas for the music.

Champ was sure a strong loud beat would keep everyone on track.

Sunny wanted music to be fun and silly.

Max thought they should look at a book to see all the options before making a decision.

Pal didn't mind what they played as long as everyone was happy.

Circle the monkey most like you

| Champ | Sunny | Max | Pal |

Monkey Tale 9

You Bug Me!

The monkeys spend a lot of time together and making the movie wasn't easy. In fact, at times it was down right difficult. Sometimes they just bugged each other. They all had their own ideas about how things should be done.

Max doesn't like when things are out of order. And the other monkeys needed to listen better.

Pal was getting a stomach ache. Peace and quiet would help everyone think better.

Sunny didn't understand what the problem was. After all, they had a superstar and the show should go on.

Champ wanted to be in charge. If the other monkeys wouldn't obey, there would be no movie.

Circle the monkey most like you

| Max | Pal | Sunny | Champ |

Monkey Tale 10

36

Problems in Paradise

The zookeeper came by on his rounds. His usual smile was gone. Something wasn't right. But they couldn't tell what the problem was.

Sunny tried to make the zookeeper laugh and gave him a hug so he would feel better.

Max worried that something the monkeys had done had upset the zookeeper.

Pal felt kind of sick because the zookeeper was feeling sad.

Champ knew it wasn't the monkeys' fault that the zookeeper was sad, but maybe they could help fix the problem.

Circle the monkey most like you

| Sunny | Max | Pal | Champ |

Lion on the Loose

When the zookeeper finally told them what had happened, they could understand why he was so sad and worried. A mountain lion was on the loose!

Max was terrified—what if the mountain lion got into their cage? Maybe they should hide.

Champ was ready with a plan to capture the mountain lion and get him back where he belonged.

Pal was worried and had a tummy ache. Would the other animals be okay?

Sunny got scared too, but offered to stay behind and report the news of the capture.

Monkey Tale 12

Celebrate the Capture

Everyone cheered and clapped when the news came that the mountain lion was captured. When the zookeeper brought a tub full of their favorite treats, the monkeys decided to celebrate.

Sunny was the first to suggest a costume party, since it was too late to make a movie anyway. It was so much fun to dress up!

Max could agree to the party but first wanted to count how many bananas they could each have.

Pal felt better now that everybody was happy and safe. It would be nice to watch everyone at the party.

Champ agreed to be in charge and tell people where to go and what they should do.

Circle the monkey most like you

| Sunny | Max | Pal | Champ |

Congratulations!

You have now completed the profile with your child.
Follow these instructions to score your child's choices.

After reading each page, your child will have circled the monkey most like him or her at the bottom of each page. Now transfer those choices to the score sheet. Be careful to record them in the correct columns, since the answers from each page were purposely ordered differently each time (as a control and to avoid children answering in a pattern and skewing results). After transferring answers to the score sheet, you can total the scores from each column. Older children may be able to transfer answers, but you will want to make sure to check for accuracy.

Add up the number of checkmarks for each column.

Each ✔ is worth one point. No score should be higher than 12 in any of the columns.

Generally, one score will be higher than the rest. This will most likely be your child's primary personality type. The next highest score that is elevated or nearly even with the high score is the secondary personality. The two highest scores indicate your child's personality blend. Your child may have two high scores the same. This would show your child's strong personality blend.

The secondary personality may not show up if your child's primary personality score is higher than 6. In this case, the personality blend may be found after doing the parent observation or reading the personality characteristics later in this book.

The reason for identifying a primary and secondary personality type is to help identify your child's combination of emotional needs. This will also be useful as you try to understand the differing traits which make up your child's unique personality blend or hue.

You may notice your child trying to select what she/he perceives as the "right" choice rather than what she/he would actually do. Some children do this because of their deep desire to please others or to "be good." If this is the case with your child, it may be helpful to discuss his/her selections and encourage him/her to choose what is most natural without worrying about what you would choose. The second high score may be helpful in reflecting your child's true answers.

We have added a Parent Observation Profile for more help in deciphering your child's personality type. This tool helps factor in your perceptions, as well as your child's picture story assessment choices.

This profile is not a diagnostic test to determine mental or psychological issues.

THE YOU ZOO Scoring Sheet

If your child is a reader, you may have him/her read the story aloud to you. Try to let your child make the choices by him/herself even if you feel it is not accurate. How your child sees him/herself is just as insightful as having your child correctly identify his or her personality type.

After completing the assessment, transfer the answers from each scenario into the scoring sheet columns. Place a ✓ in the column for the monkey your child chose was most like him/her. Be careful to record them in the correct columns, since the answers from each page were purposely ordered differently each time (as a control and to avoid children answering in a pattern and skewing results). After transferring answers to the score sheet, you can total the scores from each column.

Each ✓ is worth one (1) point. You should not have a score higher than 12.

It is normal for there to be some random scores in each category. What we will identify after all 12 scenarios is a pattern or preference. If all your child's scores are equal, you can have him/her do the assessment again later in the day or another day. Also, be sure to complete the Parent Observation Profile.

	Sunny	Champ	Pal	Max
Tale 1				
Tale 2				
Tale 3				
Tale 4				
Tale 5				
Tale 6				
Tale 7				
Tale 8				
Tale 9				
Tale 10				
Tale 11				
Tale 12				
Totals				

PART TWO

·············

The You Zoo

Parent Observation Profile™

Parent Observation Profile™ Instructions

We hope you had fun going through **THE YOU ZOO Picture Assessment** with your child. Our desire is that it will help you see a new facet of your child, or maybe even help explain, "Why does he do that?"

It's often difficult for children to see themselves as they really are. They may be trying to answer as they feel others expect or according to what seems right. That is why we incorporate a **Parent Observation Profile** that works in tandem with the picture assessment to help you identify your child's personality type.

The reason we feel it's so important to identify your child's personality category correctly is so you can figure out what is a natural personality trait (and how you might help him/her grow in that) and what may be potential speed bumps (and how you might navigate through that). Guiding your child is so much easier when you go with the natural flow of his/her built-in tendencies. This also helps you identify traits that may need some practice or training to master, since those may not come as naturally.

We encourage you to answer these questions as honestly and realistically as possible. All children have strengths and weaknesses. No child is perfect. Acknowledging a potential weakness does not mean your child always behaves in a particular way. It just means that on a bad day this particular behavior might be more noticeable by comparison. In the **Parent Observation Profile** there are twelve simple questions to identify basic behaviors. These questions are designed to cover strengths, struggles and emotional needs. Write the letter of your choice in the space to the right of the question on the profile. Be sure to answer every question with one response. When you have finished, simply circle the corresponding letter on the score sheet and add up the totals.

Understanding personality traits is not an exact science. It's a journey with many variables. The best way to approach understanding personalities is to be observant and flexible. As your child grows, different traits will emerge. Watch for the visible clues and adjust accordingly.

You will also find a section in this book with frequently asked questions. You may find some of your questions answered there. If after going through **THE YOU ZOO** Picture Assessment and **Parent Observation Profile**, you have further questions, feel free to contact Jami at: **jami@jamikirkbride.com.**

Parent Observation Profile™

PARENT OBSERVATIONS	CHILD'S BEHAVIOR	CHOICE
1. My child is…	a. a talker b. busy and active c. somewhat fearful and shy d. laid back and quiet	
2. When upset, my child…	a. becomes angry and reactive b. quietly withdraws and pouts c. hides or falls asleep d. starts to cry and throw fits	
3. When my child wants something, he/she…	a. hovers and hopes I can guess his/her need b. quietly taps to get my attention c. becomes overly cuddly and charming d. demands without "please" or "thank you"	
4. My child dislikes when others…	a. are upset or arguing b. don't pay attention to what he/she is doing (talking, playing, showing, etc.) c. doesn't do what he/she tells them to do d. invade his/her space and touch his/her things	
5. My child works best in an environment that is…	a. creative and fun b. active and structured c. familiar and secure d. calm and predictable	
6. My child struggles with…	a. obedience and getting along with others b. whining and complaining c. being pushed around or influenced by others d. being distracted and listening	

PARENT OBSERVATIONS	CHILD'S BEHAVIOR	CHOICE
7. My child is often…	a. thinking and fearful b. content and quiet c. bored or busy d. adventurous, curious, or possibly destructive	
8. My child often says…	a. "okay" b. "I want _____" or "I need _____" c. "I'll do it myself!" d. nothing, but hopes I can read his/her mind	
9. My child is comforted when…	a. she/he receives hugs and cuddles b. she/he is offered choices for a sense of control c. others are sensitive to her/his feelings and fears d. help is offered when she/he is overwhelmed	
10. My child responds best to discipline when…	a. it is consistent and fair b. it is calm and controlled, not overly harsh c. when there is a promise of reward d. I reassure her/him of my love	
11. My child may be too…	a. picky or fearful b. undecided or hesitant c. distracted or forgetful d. bossy or stubborn	
12. I often tell my child…	a. "Can you please hurry up." b. "You need to listen to me." c. "Slow down. Take your time." d. "You'll be okay."	

Parent Observation Profile™ Score Sheet

After making your choices, transfer them onto this chart by circling the letter you chose for each question. Total up each column – each circled letter is worth one point. You should not have a score higher than 12 in any one column. There will be random scores in each column, but there should be one category higher than the others. This is considered a primary personality trait.

	Sunny	Champ	Pal	Max
1	A	B	D	C
2	D	A	C	B
3	C	D	B	A
4	B	C	A	D
5	A	B	D	C
6	D	A	C	B
7	C	D	B	A
8	B	C	A	D
9	A	B	D	C
10	C	A	B	D
11	C	D	B	A
12	B	C	A	D
Totals				

PART THREE

· · · · · · · · · · · · · · · · ·

The You Zoo

Introducing the Personalities

You may be surprised to know that the study of personalities dates clear back to the Greek philosophers. In fact, the names you have seen in this book that may have sounded a bit strange -- Sanguine, Choleric, Melancholic, and Phlegmatic-- were the names the Greeks originally assigned. They classified people according to their differences and thought those differences were related to body fluids. We have learned a lot over the years and don't relate personalities to body fluids at all. We do, however, still use the Greek names of origin. We have modernized them with an easy-to-remember descriptor as well.

Introducing the **Playful Sanguine** Child

VISIBLE CLUES:

Chatters constantly – Expressive – Easily distracted
Affectionate – Laughs and Giggles – Loves people

KEY CHARACTERISTICS:

Strengths:
- Curious
- Energized by people
- Talkative
- Imaginative
- Eager to do everything
- Cheerful/bounces back
- Makes friends easily

Struggles:
- Distracted
- Easily bored
- Talks or shares too much
- Exaggerates the truth to a fib/lie
- Disorganized
- Overly dramatic
- Too trusting

From the Heart of the Playful Child

As a Playful Child, I love fun! Little things excite me, and I can usually make the most of any situation. Staying busy with people and fun activities make my life exciting. I like to share my thoughts and feelings. Hearing people praise me makes me feel inspired and happy. When you keep me focused and require quick and easy jobs I will function at my best.

EMOTIONAL NEEDS OF THE PLAYFUL CHILD:
- Wants attention from others
- Longs for affection-hugs, kisses, and cuddles
- Wants everyone to like him/her just as he/she is

CONTROLS BY:
- Pouring on the charm to get what she/he wants

SPEED BUMPS:
- Dislikes boring tasks or routine
- Burdened with details
- Avoids criticism
- Can't stay focused

COMMUNICATION STYLE OF THE Playful Child

- Expressive with body and face
- Exaggerates
- Laughs a lot
- Speaks before thinking
- Colorful stories
- Repeats stories over and over
- Open body language
- Talks to anyone/anywhere
- Uses lots of touch
- Dramatic

TIPS FOR DISCIPLINING A Playful Child

- Time outs are usually effective
- Taking away privileges or opportunities for fun can also work
- Can usually be redirected or refocused with kind reminders
- Motivate with simple, fun rewards or special activities

LEARNING TIPS FOR THE Playful Child

- Thrives on opportunities to talk, share, show, or have an audience
- Enjoys the chance to work together with a group to generate ideas
- Will be imaginative and wants to create things
- May tend to talk excessively or get sidetracked
- Likes his/her environment to be fun, bright, and exciting

Introducing the **Powerful Choleric** Child

VISIBLE CLUES:

Determined – Self-sufficient – Busy – Risk taker
Talks with hands on hips and finger pointing

KEY CHARACTERISTICS:

Strengths:
- Natural leader
- Productive
- Daring/energetic
- Focused on task
- Competitive
- Assertive
- Self-sufficient

Struggles:
- Bossy
- Constantly on the move
- Over-confident
- Insistent/headstrong
- Argumentative
- Unsympathetic
- Disregards authority

From the Heart of the Powerful Child

As a Powerful Choleric Child, I love to be in charge! Try as I might to challenge you, I really want to know that you are strong enough to handle me. I want to do it myself. Keep me busy and be consistent. I feel good when you put me in charge of appropriate things and like sincere praise for my accomplishments. My determination may sometimes wear you down, but with your direction it will serve me well.

EMOTIONAL NEEDS OF THE POWERFUL CHILD:

- Achievement—hates being busy for no good reason
- Credit for his/her hard work
- Having a sense of control (making decisions)

CONTROLS BY:

- Fits of anger, arguing, and blaming others

SPEED BUMPS:

- Won't play games she/he can't win
- Dislikes slowing down or resting
- Doesn't function well when bored
- Becomes explosive when angry

COMMUNICATION STYLE OF THE Powerful Child

- Uses finger pointing for emphasis
- Boldly opinionated
- Uses facts to make a point
- Gives commands, forgets to request
- Speaks for others
- Cuts others off
- Speaks quickly and boldly
- May lack tact or thoughtfulness
- Places hands on hips
- Sticks to their point and is insistent

TIPS FOR DISCIPLINING A Powerful Child

- Avoid dealing with him/her in anger, it only escalates the situation
- Be firm, consistent, and in control – be the BOSS!
- Assign extra tasks instead of time-outs, but make it matter to him/her
- Can motivate by giving a sense of control—achieved by offering two choices, both being OK with you.

LEARNING TIPS FOR THE Powerful Child

- Thrives on opportunities to be in charge or lead the pack
- Enjoys being challenged and getting things done
- Will function best if given options and allowed to have some choices
- May tend to take over in a group or come on too strong
- Likes his/her environment to be strong (clear boundaries and competent leaders)

Introducing the **Proper Melancholic** Child

VISIBLE CLUES:

Serious expressions – Limited body gestures – Studious
Cautious – Shy - Private with thoughts and plans

KEY CHARACTERISTICS:

Strengths:
- Thinks deeply
- Dutiful and responsible
- Perfectionist
- Artistically inclined
- Faithful friend
- Analytical
- Intense

Struggles:
- Becomes critical of others
- Easily discouraged
- Moody and fearful
- Overly self-conscious
- Easily disappointed by others
- Frustrates others by being picky
- Selfish

From the Heart of the Proper Child

As a Proper Melancholic Child, I like when things are done right. I want others to be as careful and courteous as I am. Some of the things I observe make me sad or upset. The best way to help me is to be sensitive to my feelings and don't make fun of me. I can be easily overwhelmed with things that are not as perfect as I would like them to be. Understanding and support for my wishes make me feel secure and loved. I am good at monitoring my schedule and need little direction from you.

EMOTIONAL NEEDS OF THE PROPER CHILD:
- Private personal space to call his/her own
- Support and understanding from those in charge
- Quiet—separation from noise and clutter
- Time to think through changes and plans

CONTROLS BY:
- Moodiness, pouting, and withdrawal

SPEED BUMPS:
- Little things become big issues
- Derailed by noise and clutter
- Doesn't want to be cheered up
- Becomes overwhelmed by deadlines

COMMUNICATION STYLE OF THE Proper Child

- Very private about life and self
- Uses touch sparingly
- Few and cautious gestures
- Thinks and then speaks
- Accurate with details
- Holds back information
- Good writer and artist
- Good listener
- Uses the silent treatment - pouts
- Shares desires when feeling safe and secure

TIPS FOR DISCIPLINING A Proper Child

- Provide a chance to re-do behavior without coming on too strong
- Will respond well to time outs and redirection
- Sensitive to correction…be fair and consistent
- Can be motivated by quiet time alone to re-energize and think

LEARNING TIPS FOR THE Proper Child

- Thrives on projects that have steps, details, and a clear outcome
- Enjoys being precise and working for the best results
- Will function best if given plenty of time to do work (re-check work too)
- May be quickly discouraged with group members who don't work as precisely
- Likes their environment to be orderly, quiet, and free of distraction

Introducing the **Peaceful Phlegmatic** Child

VISIBLE CLUES:

Easy going – Quiet –- Relaxed - Gentle
Likes to tease – Good sense of humor

- -

KEY CHARACTERISTICS:

Strengths:

- Easily amused
- Agreeable
- Dependable
- Requires little discipline
- Likes to listen more than talk
- Compliant
- Plays well with others

Struggles:

- Uninvolved
- Doesn't always speak honestly
- Easily manipulated by others
- Quiet will of iron
- Avoids work
- Gets lost in the shuffle
- Hard to motivate

From the Heart of the Peaceful Child

As a Peaceful Child, I like things to be easy and enjoyable. I am not easily angered, nor do I get overly excited. When things are calm and smooth, life feels good. I can go with the flow, but will probably wear out before others do. With a little bit of down time to relax and just "be", I will be ready to go again. Feeling safe and secure brings out the best in me. With your loving encouragement, we will have a peaceful and good time together.

EMOTIONAL NEEDS OF THE PROPER CHILD:

- Adequate time for relaxation and sleep
- Worth—praise for who he/she is, not what he/she does
- Peace and quiet—lack of stress or tension

CONTROLS BY:

- Procrastinating until you do it for him/her

SPEED BUMPS:

- Dislikes conflict or confrontation
- Avoids making decisions or taking initiative
- Easily overwhelmed by extra work
- Resists being in charge

COMMUNICATION STYLE OF THE *Peaceful Child*

- Limited and relaxed gestures
- May appear uninvolved
- Exhibits a calming presence
- Fearful of interfering
- Dry sense of humor
- Slow and steady pace
- Soft voice
- Relaxed body language
- May give opinion only if asked
- Speaks if it really matters

TIPS FOR DISCIPLINING THE *Peaceful Child*

- Redirect behavior before things get tense and uncomfortable
- Allow a chance to re-do the behavior the right way
- Time outs are generally effective, since she/he hates confrontation
- Can be motivated by the promise of down time to regroup and not be on the go

LEARNING TIPS FOR THE *Peaceful Child*

- Thrives on projects that are short, simple, and easy to accomplish
- Enjoys working in short spurts, but needs help staying engaged
- Will function best on large projects with a partner or in a group
- May become easily overwhelmed or tired even when having fun
- Likes their environment to be easy going and free of tension

Keys to Understanding the Personalities

- Each personality is special and important. There is no personality that is better than another or worse than another. Just like the colors in a crayon box, they each "color" things in a different way and are very important!

- The traits listed are strength-based. That means that even though we all have both strengths and struggles, it's just a matter of modifying a strength. Struggles aren't something that we can't learn to adjust. After all, struggles are just strengths taken to an extreme or using just a little too much of the strength!

- This is not intended to put anyone in a box. Rather it gives an idea of what might be a natural tendency and what might need to be practiced or learned. Your child wasn't born able to tie his shoe, but that doesn't mean that he won't or can't learn. Your child can also develop strengths and diminish struggles.

- One person doesn't usually have all the listed traits, just some of them. And one area is bound to show more similarity than the others.

- People are usually a combination of two personality types described in boxes next to each other. So, if you find it hard to choose between two…those might be the combination.

- Sometimes children perceive themselves differently than a parent perceives them. This doesn't need to create tension. Their perceptions will help you understand how they want to grow and learn.

The True You

PLAYFUL SANGUINE

The Noise Maker—Sunny

Strengths	Struggles
Curious	Distracted
Energized by people	Easily bored
Talkative	Shares too much
Imaginative	Exaggerates/fibs
Eager to do things	Disorganized
Cheerful/bounce back	Overly dramatic
Makes friends easily	Too trusting

Needs
Attention from others
Longs for affection
Wants to be liked by everyone
Wants approval even when wrong

"I must have some excitement!"

POWERFUL CHOLERIC

The Plan Maker—Champ

Strengths	Struggles
Natural leader	Bossy
Productive	Constantly on the move
Daring/energetic	Over confident
Focused on task	Insistent/headstrong
Competitive	Argumentative
Assertive	Unsympathetic
Self-sufficient	Disregards authority

Needs
Achievement
Credit for work
Having sense of control (make decisions)
Support for ideas and plans

"I must have some control!"

PEACEFUL PHLEGMATIC

The Peace Maker—Pal

Strengths	Struggles
Easily amused	Uninvolved
Agreeable	Holds back truth
Dependable	Easily manipulated
Needs little discipline	Quiet will of iron
Likes to listen	Avoids work
Compliant	Gets lost in shuffle
Plays well with others	Hard to motivate

Needs
Time for relaxation and sleep
Praise for who she/he is not what she/he does
Lack of tension and stress
Acknowledgement of contributions

"I must have some rest!"

PROPER MELANCHOLIC

The Rule Maker—Max

Strengths	Struggles
Thinks deeply	Critical of others
Dutiful/responsible	Easily discouraged
Perfectionist	Moody/fearful
Artistically inclined	Overly self conscious
Faithful friend	Disappointed by others
Analytical	Frustrates others/picky
Intense	Selfish

Needs
Space to call his/her own
Support from those in charge
Separation from noise and clutter
Time to think through changes/plans

"I must have some order!"

Understanding Who I Am

(For use with younger children)

 Color the Playful square YELLOW

 Color the Powerful square RED

 Color the Peaceful square GREEN

 Color the Proper square BLUE

Put an X in the box that had the most answers from your score sheet.

Which one are you? _____

What word do you like best about yourself? _____

Playful Sanguine
Sunny--The Noise Maker

Talkative, Imaginative, Cheerful

"I must have some excitement!"

Powerful Choleric
Champ--The Plan Maker

Confident, Determined, Energetic

"I must have some control!"

Peaceful Phlegmatic
Pal--The Peace Maker

Gentle, Agreeable, Relaxed

"I must have some rest!"

Proper Melancholic
Max--The Rule Maker

Responsible, Careful, Serious

"I must have some order!"

A View of the You Zoo

(For use with older children)

As you look over your score sheet, you will see that you selected more of one particular monkey's choices than another. Which monkey did you have the most answers like?

_____

Look for the title of the box that matches that monkey. What is the personality type found in that same box?

_____

As you look over the traits in the four squares, which one feels or sounds most like you?

_____

If the box is the same as the highest column on your score sheet, this is probably your primary personality. If the box that feels and sounds most like you is different than the one on your score sheet, this is probably your primary and secondary personality combination. Everyone is a combination of two squares, with usually one more like us than the other.

It is helpful to see how the parent observation form score fits with your results. Usually, the two results are very similar. If, however, your score and your parent's score differ greatly, that is okay. This can be a good thing to talk about. Sometimes the way you see yourself is different than the way others see you. Maybe together you can look at the four squares and find the two that are most like you. And remember...no one is wrong. This is just figuring it out together.

What are three traits in the strengths column that you like about yourself? These are probably things that come easy for you:

_____

_____

_____

Usually our struggles are a strength taken too far. What is one trait that you see in the struggles column of your personality's square? And what is one way you can get that trait back to a strength?

_____

_____

There are some other things we can learn from looking at the four squares. This information might help you if you are still struggling to find your combination of two squares, or your primary and secondary personality type.

The top two squares show **Playful Sunny** and **Powerful Champ**. They are both extroverts. That is just a fancy way to say they are energized by being with people. The bottom two squares show **Peaceful Pal** and **Proper Max**. They are both introverts. And that is just a fancy way to say they are energized by quiet time or time spent alone. What about you? Are you energized by people or by quiet or alone time? If you had a horrible week at school and you were really frustrated, what would you want to do—be with a group of friends or be home doing something quiet?

_____

The two squares on the left side show personalities who think more about people than about what needs to be done. The two squares on the right show personalities who think more about what needs to be done than the people involved. What about you? Do you focus more on what you need to get done or find yourself worrying more about how things are going with other people?

_____

As you look at the traits on the chart, there might be good traits that don't fall in your box. But there are no limits to what you can learn and develop. The traits outside your box might be very important to learn. Take responsible for example. That might come easy for someone who is a **Proper Max**. But it is a trait that all of us need at times. Other personalities just might need practice to become more responsible. Find another trait that is not in your box but that you would like to have. How could you develop that trait?

_____

_____

What is the best thing you have learned about yourself while doing **The You Zoo**?

_____

_____

REMEMBER:
You are special and unique just the way you are!

67

PART FOUR

The You Zoo

Adult Personality Profile

Instructions for the Adult Personality Profile

The real value in understanding personality types is how these traits affect relationships. So understanding your child's personality is only part of the process. Now it's your turn to identify your personality type and see how that affects the way you approach parenting.

This short, easy adult personality profile is designed to help you identify your personality traits, and how they line up with those of your child. The rest of this book is focused on helping you maximize your parenting skills through easy to understand charts, points, and tips.

Science has found that our personality traits are encoded in our DNA. We get our personalities from our parents, the same way we get our body build, eye color, and skin tone. In other words certain traits are hard-wired right into our behavior.

Each personality type has its own set of strengths, struggles, and emotional needs. Strengths are things we are naturally good at doing, struggles are things that we have to work at overcoming, and emotional needs are the desires or invisible forces that compel us toward a certain behavior or way of thinking.

After completing the personality profile you may find you have a score in each category. What we are looking for is the pattern or preference. One personality type should stand out more than the others – indicating this is most likely your primary personality. You may also have two scores that are equal. This just shows you have a strong personality blend.

If your scores come out even in all four categories, do the profile again or have someone take it with you. If your score still comes out even, read over the emotional needs list for each personality and eliminate the ones that don't feel right to you. After the answer key, you will find a chart listing some of the strengths, struggles, and emotional needs for each personality. Look them over to see if you can tell which one you identify with most. What you should find is one personality's list will feel better to you than the others. This is most likely your primary personality type.

If after taking the profile you have any questions, please feel free to send your questions and comments to: **kathryn@personalityprinciples.com**

Which personality style is the best?
The one that is living in their strengths!

Personality Principles Adult Profile™

Directions: Read the four statements carefully. Put a circle around the number that is MOST like you.

You may find that in some sections, none of the answers apply and in other sections more than one applies, please pick one answer in each section the first time you do the profile. If you are having trouble making a choice, ask for help from someone who knows you well

---

A

1. I don't mind being the focus of attention, even around people I don't know.

2. I am a private person. I don't think it's necessary to tell everyone my business.

3. I like to be the leader because I have really good ideas of what can be accomplished.

4. People like me because I'm kind and gentle, saying nice things at the right time.

B

5. I like to make decisions because I'm usually right.

6. Decisions are hard to make. I would rather let someone else decide for me.

7. Decisions are easy for me to make because I have the freedom to change my mind.

8. I don't make decisions quickly. I want to study the facts first, so I make the right choice.

C

9. When people are arguing and yelling, I feel physical pain in my stomach.

10. Hugs are healing. I think everyone needs a hug, so I love to hug everyone.

11. I take time to think things through. I wish people would understand why this is important.

12. I like to finish my work fast. Getting things done feels good to me.

D

13. I love to talk and tell funny stories so people will laugh.

14. When I talk, people know I'm in charge.

15. I like to think out what I'm going to say ahead of time. I don't want to be embarrassed.

16. I like to listen more than talk because it's nice when you listen to what others have to say.

E

17   My feelings get hurt easily. I think people talk about me behind my back.

18   It bothers me when things keep changing. I like knowing what to expect before it happens.

19   I think it's sad to only have one best friend. I have many best friends.

20   It drives me crazy when things don't run right. That's why I like being the boss.

F

21   If I wait long enough, someone else might do it for me.

22   When my friends and family hurt my feelings, I separate myself from them for a while.

23   I lose track of my things-shoes, keys, jewelry. Time gets away from me too.

24   When I think things are stupid or wrong, I just take over and fix it even if it's not my job.

G

25   I love doing things the fun way!

26   I want things done my way!

27   I like to do things the easy way.

28   The best way is to do it the right way.

H

29   I am a good listener and don't demand my own way.

30   In an emergency, I can think fast and react quickly, without having to think about it.

31   It helps my brain feel organized if I write everything out on paper first.

32   I love everybody and everybody loves me!

TRANSFER YOUR ANSWERS TO THE ANSWER KEY.

Circle the same number in the boxes below that you circled in the chart on the previous page.

Each answer is worth 1 (one) point. Total each column.

Playful Sanguine	Powerful Choleric	Proper Melancholic	Peaceful Phlegmatic
1	3	2	4
7	5	8	6
10	12	11	9
13	14	15	16
19	20	17	18
23	24	22	21
25	26	28	27
32	30	31	29
TOTAL	TOTAL	TOTAL	TOTAL

Your score should not be more than (8) in any one column.

The highest score is most likely your primary personality.
The second highest score should be your secondary personality.

If you feel the category with the highest score does not fit your personality, do the profile over by putting an X through the box that is NOT like you. Add up your X totals on the lines below. You can eliminate that category. Do this again and eliminate another category. Of the two categories left, one should be your primary personality and the other your secondary personality category.

TOTAL_____   _____   _____   _____

If neither way helped you identify your category, have a friend or family member take the profile for you.

The Personality Principles assessment profile is not a test or diagnostic instrument.
Its intended use is to help identify your primary personality traits.

PLAYFUL SANGUINE	POWERFUL CHOLERIC
### The Talker	### The Doer

<table>
<tr><th>PLAYFUL SANGUINE</th><th>POWERFUL CHOLERIC</th></tr>
<tr><td>

The Talker

Loud voice • Loud clothing • Curious
Open mouth • Open life - TMI
Talks with hands • Intriguing life
Wide eyed • Loves attention

Strengths	Struggles
Loves people	Gets bored easily
Makes friends easily	Can't say "no"
Exciting storyteller	Talks too much
Good salesman	Lacks focus

Emotional Needs
Attention from all
Affection, hugs, kisses, touching
Approval of every deed
Acceptance "as is"

Controls By: Charm and laughter

</td><td>

The Doer

Natural leader • Decisive • Directional
Likes to get things done
Always on the move
Finger pointing while talking

Strengths	Struggles
Natural born leader	Over confident
Usually right	Can't say "I'm sorry"
Loves a challenge	Quits when losing
Problem fixer	Wants to be the boss

Emotional Needs
Accomplishment
Support and loyalty
Sense of control
Appreciation for service

Controls By: Angry outbursts

</td></tr>
<tr><th>PEACEFUL PHLEGMATIC</th><th>PROPER MELANCHOLIC</th></tr>
<tr><td>

The Watcher

Easygoing • Quiet • Light on his/her feet
Blends in • Comfortable clothing
Steady worker • Flexible • Kind
Likes to make others feel good

Strengths	Struggles
Steady, reliable	Dislikes change
Good listener	Uninvolved
Calm, witty, kind	Avoids conflict
Has few enemies	Will of iron

Emotional Needs
Peace and quiet
Feelings of worth
Lack of stress - sleep
Respect for who he/she is

Controls By: Procrastination

</td><td>

The Thinker

Private • Proper • Sensitive
Organizes using charts, graphs and lists
Not flashy • Artistic/musical
Deep thinker • Quiet

Strengths	Struggles
Analytical	Super perfectionist
Works well alone	Loner
Planner	Stunted under pressure
Organized	Overly sensitive - selfish

Emotional Needs
Space to be alone,
Silence - no people
Sensitivity to feelings
Understanding

Controls By: Moodiness

</td></tr>
</table>

PART FIVE

The You Zoo

Personality Parenting Tips

Parenting Tips for the **Playful** Parent

PARENT CHARACTERISTICS:

Strengths:
- Energetic
- Warm
- Enthusiastic
- Approachable
- Forgiving
- Cheerleader

Struggles:
- Too loud
- Superficial
- Impulsive
- Self-centered
- Forgetful/unreliable
- Distracted

> You will make many special and exciting memories for your child. While taking time for fun and activities, don't forget to focus on other important parts of life . . . completing tasks, remembering details, and taking a rest. Be sure to give your child time to express him/herself and be noticed too. Children need to feel that you are capable and can handle the role of parent and not just a playmate.

RELATIONSHIP STRENGTHS:

With a Playful Child

- Fun, energetic, and exciting combination – best friends!
- Both child and parent share the need to laugh, talk, and have fun.
- You will share wonderful adventures like shopping, parties, and playing—making even small incidents into great stories.

With a Powerful Child

- You and your child are both energized by being with people.
- Your enthusiasm is the wind beneath this child's wings, because a powerful child wants to soar as high as he/she can.
- Your optimism will help your child overcome the temptation to quit when she/he doesn't always win.

With a Proper Child

- This child will do well, because of your ability to forgive and forget.
- Your activities, if not too extreme, will help your child experience fun.
- Your child's emotional need for understanding will sharpen your listening and reaction skills.

With a Peaceful Child

- Your fun approach to life will be appreciated but with less energy.
- Your child's need for down time can give you rest you don't usually take.
- This child will help you understand that fun can be quiet and calm, like coloring or playing board games.

PARENTING TIPS FOR SPEED BUMPS:

 With a Playful Child

- Be careful that your desire to be part of your child's life doesn't turn into you taking over their friendships.

- Allow your child time in the limelight too. You both like to be center stage.

- Understand that playfuls love to laugh, joke, and tell stories but will be hesitant if someone bigger than them already fills that role.

 With a Powerful Child

- Be consistent with your commitments and rules to help your child know that you are strong enough to handle his/her plans and demands.

- Realize your need for fun may not match your child's desire for accomplishment.

- Remember your fun activities may irritate your child. After all, powerful children don't want to look bad or play games they can't win.

 With a Proper Child

- Protect your child's privacy which helps him/her feel loved and protected. You love to talk and share stories, but this child doesn't want to be the topic of your stories and jokes.

- Be sensitive to your child's feelings when dealing with meltdowns – never tease about his/her fears, or make light of his/her dreams.

- Accept the fact that silly stories and games don't work as well as quiet understanding.

 With a Peaceful Child

- Be aware that your energy level can quickly overwhelm your child.

- Ask your child about his/her opinion or feelings since she/he won't just offer them.

- Help your child break down overwhelming tasks into smaller parts and voice his/her opinions. You will be pleased to see your child come to life.

Parenting Tips for the **Powerful** Parent:

PARENT CHARACTERISTICS:

Strengths:
- Productive
- Competitive
- Multi-tasker
- Purposeful
- Problem solver
- Organizes people

Struggles:
- Overbearing
- Argumentative
- Arrogant
- Offensive
- Controlling/bossy
- Disregards authority

> You will undoubtedly teach your child a lot about work ethics and being active. Remember to take time to have fun and relax. Become observant of the details in their lives. Your child will be sensitive to your thoughts and actions . . . remember to think before you act or speak! Be sure to give your child time to grow, learn, and try new things on his/her own. You do not need to fix all their problems—struggle is a part of maturing.

RELATIONSHIP STRENGTHS:

With a Playful Child

- This is an energetic combination as both child and parent want to be involved in different activities and stay busy.

- Both you and your child enjoy being with people.

- This child can help you enjoy the fun side of life and make you laugh.

With a Powerful Child

- This combination could be the "dynamic duo" with super drive.

- When you are both on the same side of an issue, things will definitely get done.

- Both of you love a challenge and this can play out in sports, games, or problem solving situations such as math, science, or engineering.

With a Proper Child

- This combination can be one of teamwork and inventive progress.

- As the parent, you provide the forward movement and the child will provide the details to make things work more smoothly.

- Both parent and child share the ability to focus on the task at hand.

With a Peaceful Child

- This child is very willing to follow the parent's lead, making life easier.

- Both parent and child can be great problem solvers.

- Learning to do things at this child's slower pace will help you learn patience.

PARENTING TIPS FOR THE SPEED BUMPS:

With a Playful Child –

- Give your child grace for not staying on task. This helps your child with stress levels, self-esteem, and feeling loved.

- Remind yourself to relax a little and have fun.

- Interact in ways that are not always intense and productive--laugh, joke, and even play games that are just crazy.

With a Powerful Child –

- Offer opportunities to choose and make decisions, making sure all options offered are OK with you.

- Make boundaries clear--she/he wants to know that you are in control.

- Stay calm. Powerful children do not respond well to angry commands.

With a Proper Child

- Understand your proper child's need to check, recheck, and even redo. Perfection or near perfection is important to him/her.

- Encourage him/her gently to accept some mistakes as being part of life.

- Affirm --the proper child will be easily discouraged when she/he feels he/she has not met your standards.

With a Peaceful Child

- Make an effort to be calm--your child will feel your intensity long before you are aware of it.

- Realize your determination may cause a physiological response that can essentially cause this child to shut down.

- Take a breath, slow down, and accept a slower and calmer pace.

Parenting Tips for the **Proper** Parent:

PARENT CHARACTERISTICS:

Strengths:
- Empathetic
- Analytical
- Organized
- Scheduled
- Gifted
- Reliable

Struggles:
- Fearful
- Critical/ intense
- Obsessive
- Moody
- Fragile
- Uptight

> You will work hard to maintain high standards for cleanliness, organization, and commitment. Your attention to detail can easily feel like nit-picking and can quickly discourage children. Remember that your moods can feel controlling if you don't make a conscious effort to lighten up and enjoy life with some spontaneity, direction and positive reactions.

RELATIONSHIP STRENGTHS:

With a Playful Child –
- This child will help bring enthusiasm to your organized goals.
- Your child will bring the laughter and joy while you bring the focus to the relationship.
- Your giftedness along with your child's imagination can allow great creativity.

With a Powerful Child –
- With your child's drive and your detailed plan to reach the goal, you can accomplish great things.
- You and your child are both able to focus on the task at hand.
- Your child will help drive things when you get stuck on the details or processes.

With a Proper Child –
- This combination will be one of deep and careful thinking.
- Your child's need for personal space is the same as yours.
- You will both be able to see the details and understand their importance.

With a Peaceful Child –
- This combination is generally easy and peaceful.
- Your child desires to make you happy, and is willing to follow your way of doing things as long as you are nice about it.
- You both share the desire for quiet harmony.

PARENTING TIPS FOR THE SPEED BUMPS:

 With a Playful Child –

- Accept that details important to you don't even occur to your child.

- Remember fun is messy and perfection gets in the way of fun. Your child's need for fun will collide with your need for being proper.

- Be willing to be active. While you prefer a schedule and a single focus your child will want to do everything, with no desire to practice any of it.

 With a Powerful Child –

- Empower this child with appropriate challenges. Let your child learn by doing, even if she/he fails.

- Remind yourself there is more than one right way to do things. This child will cooperate better when she/he has options.

- Acknowledge that your child wants to get it done now and may not want to agonize over the details and research that you think are important.

 With a Proper Child –

- Understand that this child will be very sensitive to your criticism.

- Use care--you see what needs to be perfected, but make sure this child knows and feels that you love him/her even when she/he makes mistakes.

- Be careful that both of you don't feed on negative self-doubt and fears.

 With a Peaceful Child -

- Relax—your child does not share your love for analyzing details. Doing all that thinking leaves the peaceful child drained and overwhelmed.

- Realize it is easy for this child to feel internally frustrated or shut down by trying to live up to a standard that is neither natural nor desirable.

- Praise him/her for who she/he is – a good kid -- not just for what she/he can do – good behavior.

Parenting Tips for the *Peaceful* Parent:

PARENT CHARACTERISTICS:

Strengths:
- Flexible
- Witty
- Dependable/steady
- Consistent
- Patient
- Supportive

Struggles:
- Indecisive
- Sarcastic
- Unemotional
- Boring
- Spineless
- Lacks initiative

As the most flexible of the four personality types, you have the ability to exhibit traits of the other personalities when necessary. This is a great advantage when you are pushed out of your comfort zone. Push yourself to take initiative and experience some excitement. Adding new perspectives to your life enables you to raise well-rounded children. Fight the urge to always be the softie. There's nothing wrong with sticking to your guns.

RELATIONSHIP STRENGTHS:

With a Playful Child –

- This will be a pleasant and light-hearted combination – full of hugs and kisses.
- Both parent and child value relationship over tasks.
- Parent and child will experience excitement and fun, especially around holidays or celebrations.

With a Powerful Child –

- This combination will help develop your inner strength.
- As opposites, you will learn to be a leader, while teaching your child the necessity of following the rules.
- This child will keep you up and moving with determination and focus.

With a Proper Child –

- This can be an accommodating combination as a parent. You are relationship focused and your child is task focused.
- You both share the need for quiet time, so naps will be a welcome idea.
- You are both energized by down time, which is time away from people.

With a Peaceful Child -

- This will be a laid back, calm, and peaceful combination.
- You will understand each other well, since you share many similarities.
- Your child will be refreshing to you, as she/he doesn't demand as much.

PARENTING TIPS FOR SPEED BUMPS:

With a Playful Child –

- Perk up -- you may be content with limited activities and excitement, but your child will not. You don't want to train him/her to be insistent to get you moving.
- Push yourself to get involved with your child's activities. Keeping an eye on your child is very important, as she/he is easily influenced for good or bad.
- Learn to be more expressive and communicate more with your child.

With a Powerful Child –

- Be firm and consistent as your child pushes to see that you really are up for the challenge of keeping him/her in line. This firmness is a safety net.
- Use your quiet will of iron to establish your position. When your child knows you mean business the battles will be easier to diffuse.
- Empower your child as you listen to him/her formulate grandiose ideas or dreams. Be sure to speak up or your silence will be taken as a yes.

With a Proper Child –

- Avoid being manipulated by his/her moods. Give space and silence, but being left alone too long will not help resolve feelings.
- Help your child learn that "less than perfect can still be very good."
- Be sensitive to the things that stress out a proper child, such as problems and details. What may look like too much work to you may be very important to your child.

With a Peaceful Child –

- Communicate truthfully about your feelings and desires. Don't just leave things to be understood.
- Get moving—it's easy to let this child sit and watch TV, but it's up to you to get him/her involved in activities that round out experiences.
- Stretch yourself to make decisions, show initiative, and speak up. Your child will share the same hesitancy and will need your good example.

PART SIX

The You Zoo

Frequently Asked Questions

Frequently Asked Questions

Q *When did people start talking about personalities?*

A You may be surprised to know that the study of personalities dates clear back to the Greek philosophers. In fact, the names you have seen in this book that may have sounded a bit strange -- Sanguine, Choleric, Melancholic, and Phlegmatic-- were the names the Greeks originally assigned. They classified people according to their differences and thought those differences were related to body fluids. We have learned a lot over the years and don't relate personalities to body fluids at all. We do, however, still use the Greek names of origin and have modernized them with an easy-to-remember descriptor as well.

Q *How does this personality system compare with other systems?*

A Believe it or not, there are hundreds of personality systems in use. Some systems are more widely recognized than others. Many, though, are complicated to interpret or understand or the results are too easily forgotten. Several systems use four different types. These systems may use colors, animals, or names to distinguish personality types. Our system incorporates original Greek terms, easily remembered descriptors, and colors. It is acceptable to use any of those, whichever is easiest for you to remember.

This is one of the few systems that actually references emotional needs. We feel incorporation of emotional needs helps us understand the motivation behind a behavior. This is one of the most user-friendly versions of personality study. After just one hour, people are able to relate this knowledge to themselves and others and use it in a meaningful way.

Q *How do the colors relate to the names/titles?*

A We relate yellow to the Playful Sanguine—bright and sunny. Red relates to the Powerful Choleric—quick and purposeful as a fire truck. Blue relates to the Proper Melancholic—a deep thinker who reminds us of the deep blue ocean. Green relates to the Peaceful Phlegmatic—who reminds us of a quiet green meadow. Some people have a better memory for the colors. Others will prefer the descriptive word or Greek title. Any form is acceptable.

Q *Does everybody fit nicely into one of the personality types?*

A No, actually, it's not that simple. Each person is a combination of two personality types. Those two are usually a combination of two adjoining boxes (as you look at the personality quadrants), with the opposite boxes representing opposing personalities. One would be considered the primary personality type and the other a secondary personality.

Q *Do you really think it is a good idea to classify children and put them in a box?*

A That is exactly the opposite of what this system attempts to do. We don't want any child to be put in a box. Understanding more about a child allows you to help that child stretch, grow, and become all she/he can be. And when children understand themselves better, they feel more competent, capable, and accepting of themselves. So, it is our belief that when children learn about personalities they are acquiring keys to grow and stretch themselves and better relate to those around them. That is freeing.

Q *How will I know if my child's answers are accurate?*

A Your child will choose one monkey more often than another. But children will still have some answers that fit into other columns. If you are helping your child take the assessment, you may hear some of his/her thought process as she/he makes selections. You can also ask about the responses. But remember, you will want to do this in a very non-threatening way. Sometimes the way children perceive themselves gives us insight into their world and how they may wish they were perceived.

Q *What if my child's scoring and the parent observation scoring do not agree?*

A That would not be uncommon. In fact, sometimes, differing scores may indicate the primary and secondary types. So in this situation, you would see your scoring results would be two boxes that touch. Look at the personality traits as they are listed and described and the "True You" quick reference quadrants to figure out which personality type appears to fit most closely with your child. This may help you decipher the primary (or more dominant) personality and the secondary personality(present but not as obvious).

Q *What if I have two children with the same personality result but they don't seem the same?*

A That would be expected. After all, no two individuals are exactly alike. Let's say, for example, that we are talking about two Playful Sanguines. One may be a Playful Sanguine and Peaceful Phlegmatic combination, while the other could be a Playful Sanguine and Powerful Choleric combination. These two combinations would present very differently, as the Playful/Peaceful would be a more toned down Playful Sanguine. The Playful/Powerful combination would be a louder and more extroverted Playful Sanguine. Additionally, birth order will play a role in the way a personality presents. That's why it is helpful to think of personality types as a color wheel with many hues and shades to be expressed—not just four.

Q *It has been said that birth order affects a personality. Is there anything else that impacts a personality?*

A There are many factors including: parents with strong personalities, religious beliefs, moral beliefs, or gender. As we have said, thinking about personalities as a color wheel may help you imagine the possible blends of uniqueness and similarity.

Q *What if the results of the children's assessment and parent profile are not adjoining boxes, but are opposite each other?*

A This is where you will do some careful thinking. One of two things may be happening. First, the child (or parent in some cases) may be answering as she/he wishes it were, or what she/he thinks would be more acceptable or right. Second, there are occasions in which a dominant personality in a parent may put pressure on a child to adapt his/her natural tendency to accommodate the parental expectations. In this situation, a child is learning behaviors that may make a situation more workable. In this case, we would say there is a primary, a secondary, and a learned personality. A learned personality is not necessarily a bad thing. There may be occasions in life where it is helpful or useful. But as parents we hope that we can accept our children as they are and help them accept themselves as well.

Q *What if there are three boxes that all sound like me or my child?*

A Usually when this happens, it includes the lower left hand quadrant (Peaceful Phlegmatic). If this is true in your situation, that is not surprising. The Peaceful Phlegmatic is often times referred to as the chameleon or all-purpose personality who adapts to what a situation needs. There are also times that reflect a primary personality, a secondary personality, and learned behavior. This may mean that you and/or your child has functioned beyond what comes naturally or has learned additional traits to be effective.

Q *Can I be a combination of all four?*

A Simply put…no. Only the Creator of the Universe could be that perfect! You may have random traits that fall in other quadrants or types, but you are looking for which type has the most traits like you.

Q *What if I don't have all the listed strengths or struggles?*

A It would be rare that someone would have every trait on the lists. Remember, these are traits that come naturally. You may possess five in one and one or two in each of the other three, but the thing that you would pay attention to would be the personality type that is most like you. And remember, while it can be hard to look at the list of struggles and admit to any of those, it is perfectly normal for you and your child to have some areas of struggle. That is just part of being human.

Q *Is it a good thing or bad thing that my personality is the same as my child?*

A It is neither good nor bad, it just is! In many ways you will understand your child well. His/her thoughts, attitudes, and actions probably fall close to what you might think or do. You might even be able to predict how she/he will react or reason. On the flip side, some of the things you might not necessarily appreciate about yourself might be observable in your child as well. So really, it will only be what you make it. Let it be a positive experience for both of you.

Q *My child and I are total opposites. What does that mean?*

A The good news is that you see things in different ways. And that will be both challenging and insightful. The better news is that you will bring two totally different approaches together and get a lot of ground covered in thought and action. You have your bases covered. And just as when parent and child are similar—it will be what you make it. Let it be a good opportunity for both of you.

Q *What personality is the best personality?*

A The personality living in strengths is the best. In other words, no personality type is better or worse than another. Each has a different set of traits and natural tendencies and all make life interesting. Each individual has strengths and struggles. So really, any personality is wonderful when you operate within your strengths and modify the areas where you struggle. Just like all the crayons in a box look different but add something different to a picture, so do our personalities. Each of us has much to contribute to the fullness of life.

Q *What if I don't like my personality?*

A We have been asked this before. And for every one who asks it, there are probably five more who wanted to! It can be very easy to look at the other personality traits and wish you were more of another or less of what you are. That might just be part of our human nature -- always thinking the grass is greener on the other side of the fence. When we learn to accept and appreciate who we are then we can live our lives in a genuine fashion and feel fulfilled. Good things happen when we understand ourselves and others better.

Q *What is a personality trainer? And can you help someone who doesn't have one?*

A That one always makes us laugh. If it were only that easy! Everyone has a personality. Some may not be using their personality strengths and may be exhibiting more of their struggles instead. As trainers, we go through an education and certification process to learn about the history, the assessments, and the numerous applications of the personality system. Trainers then use that information to help educate and encourage others to gain personal insight and improve relationships. Through workshops, presentations, and written literature, trainers seek to help others use their new found knowledge of personalities in all aspects of their lives and relationships. Many report that this information is life-changing!

Q *I'm just not sure that the results are accurate. Is there any way to double check?*

A We suggest first that you complete the children's assessment, the parent observation form, and the adult personality profile. We also recommend that you read each of the personality introductions and look over the chart that has the personality in the four boxes to see which one sounds most like your child. If you are still concerned, you can have you child take the assessment in another way. Have them choose the monkey that is least like them. Total those results as well. Usually, this result is the box directly opposite the personality type that they are. Or as you look at the chart, find the box you know with certainty they are not. Locate the square opposite that one and that is most likely the primary personality type.

Q *Doesn't knowing one's personality allow them to use that as a crutch and think they can't do anything about it...that's just way they are?*

A Anyone can choose to use personal insight as a crutch. But what we as trainers encourage people to do is consider this information as just a piece of the puzzle. How can this information help you grow, learn, and improve relationships? If you know that your personality struggle might include being overbearing, how can you learn to soften your approach? If you realize that you can be perceived as uninvolved, how can you engage in a more meaningful way? In this way, you can challenge yourself in your growth and not just sit idle in the knowledge you gain.

Q *Would this information be helpful for my child's teacher to know?*

A Absolutely! That is why we are trying to get this product into schools. We believe it could change the way educators approach students and how they maximize a child's learning potential. We have even tested this assessment in a Blue Ribbon Award school. The students and teachers loved it and were eager to put the information to use. If you think your child's school would be interested, please pass along this information. We are willing to do consultations with and programs for schools.

Frequently Asked Questions copyright © 2011 by Jami Kirkbride

Speaker ~Trainer ~ Counselor

You will find **Jami Kirkbride** nestled on the quiet prairie of a Wyoming ranch where she is inspired to write and speak from her daily experiences. Her loving family (including husband Jeff and children, Taylor, Carter, Jackson, Savannah, and Jayden) provides her with many opportunities to enjoy the unique personalities and how they color life.

When Jami is not knee-deep in parenting issues, she finds time to help others improve their relationships, gain new perspectives, and make the most of life's opportunities. The Parenting with Personality Seminars she conducts help parents feel refreshed, equipped, and eager to parent in positive and purposeful ways. Her colorful examples, practical tools, and relatable style enable others to appreciate personality differences and improve relationships.

Jami is a Licensed Professional Counselor, speaker, author and Certified Personality Trainer. She received a Bachelor's degree in Psychology and a Master's degree in Counseling from the University of Northern Colorado. Jami is a contributing author to numerous books, including Pearl Girls, The Mommy Diaries, Laundry Tales, Cup of Comfort Devotional for Mothers and Daughters, Daily Devotions for Writers, and When God Steps In. She has been published with MOPS International, Discipleship Journal, Focus on Your Child, and CBN.com.

Are you looking for a rejuvenated approach to parenting? Jami can help you gain a healthy perspective on individual differences, develop positive communication, and build relationships that are life-changing. She will help couples, families, work places, community groups, and individuals through:

Back: Jami and Taylor
Middle: Carter, Jeff and Jackson
Front: Savannah and Jayden

- Workshops or presentations
- Retreats
- Parenting with Personality Seminars
- Private consulting

Visit **JamiKirkbride.com** for booking information and products.

Trainer ~ Speaker ~ Coach

Kathryn Robbins is a Certified Life Coach, Personality Trainer, Speaker, and author who loves empowering people by helping them unlock their potential through understanding their natural personality's strengths, struggles and emotional needs.

Kathryn is the President of Personality Principles LLC. She has helped incorporate the idea of understanding personality tendencies into numerous types of professions such as teaching, coaching, counseling, sales, and management through:

- Workshops or seminars
- Online training
- Keynote conference speaker
- Coaching

As the young mother of five sons, Kathryn prayed for tools to help raise her sons, better her marriage, and overcome her personal struggles. Her prayer was answered when she listened to a recording by Florence Littauer explaining personality types. Kathryn applied the information to her life and later received training from Florence, which lead to becoming the Director of The Personalities for CLASServices for several years. Kathryn is a contributing author to Wired That Way.

Minnesota is "home," but she lives in St. Louis, Missouri with her husband Steve and three of their five sons. She is grandma to one darling granddaughter (finally a girl!) who loves all things bright and shiny.

Granddaughter Jenna (parents – Drew & Abi)

From left to right: Garrett, Brett & Nicole, Drew & Abigail, Katie & Ryan, Kelly & Eric, Kathryn & Steve

For further information about Personality Principles or Kathryn's speaking topics, visit her website **www.personalityprinciples.com.**

While there, feel free to take our **FREE 5 minute** personality assessment profile.

Additional YOU ZOO Scoring Sheet

If your child is a reader, you may have him/her read the story aloud to you. Try to let your child make the choices by him/herself even if you feel it is not accurate. How your child sees him/herself is just as insightful as having your child correctly identify his/her personality type.

After completing the assessment, transfer the answers from each scenario into the scoring sheet columns. Place a ✔ in the column for the monkey your child chose was most like him/her. Be careful to record them in the correct columns, since the answers from each page were purposely ordered different each time (as a control and to avoid children answering in a pattern and skewing results). After transferring answers to the score sheet, you can total the scores from each column.

Each ✔ is worth one (1) point. You should not have a score higher than 12.

It is normal for there to be some random scores in each category. What we will identify after all 12 scenarios is a pattern or preference. If all your child's scores are equal, you can have him/her repeat the assessment again later in the day or another day. Also, be sure to complete the Parent Observation Profile.

	Sunny	Champ	Pal	Max
Tale 1				
Tale 2				
Tale 3				
Tale 4				
Tale 5				
Tale 6				
Tale 7				
Tale 8				
Tale 9				
Tale 10				
Tale 11				
Tale 12				
Totals				

Additional YOU ZOO Scoring Sheet

If your child is a reader, you may have him/her read the story aloud to you. Try to let your child make the choices by him/herself even if you feel it is not accurate. How your child sees him/herself is just as insightful as having your child correctly identify his/her personality type.

After completing the assessment, transfer the answers from each scenario into the scoring sheet columns. Place a ✓ in the column for the monkey your child chose was most like him/her. Be careful to record them in the correct columns, since the answers from each page were purposely ordered different each time (as a control and to avoid children answering in a pattern and skewing results). After transferring answers to the score sheet, you can total the scores from each column.

Each ✓ is worth one (1) point. You should not have a score higher than 12.

It is normal for there to be some random scores in each category. What we will identify after all 12 scenarios is a pattern or preference. If all your child's scores are equal, you can have him/her repeat the assessment again later in the day or another day. Also, be sure to complete the Parent Observation Profile.

	Sunny	Champ	Pal	Max
Tale 1				
Tale 2				
Tale 3				
Tale 4				
Tale 5				
Tale 6				
Tale 7				
Tale 8				
Tale 9				
Tale 10				
Tale 11				
Tale 12				
Totals				

Additional YOU ZOO Scoring Sheet

If your child is a reader, you may have him/her read the story aloud to you. Try to let your child make the choices by him/herself even if you feel it is not accurate. How your child sees him/herself is just as insightful as having your child correctly identify his/her personality type.

After completing the assessment, transfer the answers from each scenario into the scoring sheet columns. Place a ✔ in the column for the monkey your child chose was most like him/her. Be careful to record them in the correct columns, since the answers from each page were purposely ordered different each time (as a control and to avoid children answering in a pattern and skewing results). After transferring answers to the score sheet, you can total the scores from each column.

Each ✔ is worth one (1) point. You should not have a score higher than 12.

It is normal for there to be some random scores in each category. What we will identify after all 12 scenarios is a pattern or preference. If all your child's scores are equal, you can have him/her repeat the assessment again later in the day or another day. Also, be sure to complete the Parent Observation Profile.

	Sunny	Champ	Pal	Max
Tale 1				
Tale 2				
Tale 3				
Tale 4				
Tale 5				
Tale 6				
Tale 7				
Tale 8				
Tale 9				
Tale 10				
Tale 11				
Tale 12				
Totals				

Additional YOU ZOO Scoring Sheet

If your child is a reader, you may have him/her read the story aloud to you. Try to let your child make the choices by him/herself even if you feel it is not accurate. How your child sees him/herself is just as insightful as having your child correctly identify his/her personality type.

After completing the assessment, transfer the answers from each scenario into the scoring sheet columns. Place a ✔ in the column for the monkey your child chose was most like him/her. Be careful to record them in the correct columns, since the answers from each page were purposely ordered different each time (as a control and to avoid children answering in a pattern and skewing results). After transferring answers to the score sheet, you can total the scores from each column.

Each ✔ is worth one (1) point. You should not have a score higher than 12.

It is normal for there to be some random scores in each category. What we will identify after all 12 scenarios is a pattern or preference. If all your child's scores are equal, you can have him/her repeat the assessment again later in the day or another day. Also, be sure to complete the Parent Observation Profile.

	Sunny	Champ	Pal	Max
Tale 1				
Tale 2				
Tale 3				
Tale 4				
Tale 5				
Tale 6				
Tale 7				
Tale 8				
Tale 9				
Tale 10				
Tale 11				
Tale 12				
Totals				

Parent Observation Profile™ Score Sheet

After making your choices, transfer them onto this chart by circling the letter you chose for each question. Total up each column – each circled letter is worth one point. You should not have a score higher than 12 in any one column. There will be random scores in each column, but there should be one category higher than the others. This is considered a primary personality trait.

	Sunny	Champ	Pal	Max
1	A	B	D	C
2	D	A	C	B
3	C	D	B	A
4	B	C	A	D
5	A	B	D	C
6	D	A	C	B
7	C	D	B	A
8	B	C	A	D
9	A	B	D	C
10	C	A	B	D
11	C	D	B	A
12	B	C	A	D
Totals				

Parent Observation Profile™ Score Sheet

After making your choices, transfer them onto this chart by circling the letter you chose for each question. Total up each column – each circled letter is worth one point. You should not have a score higher than 12 in any one column. There will be random scores in each column, but there should be one category higher than the others. This is considered a primary personality trait.

	Sunny	Champ	Pal	Max
1	A	B	D	C
2	D	A	C	B
3	C	D	B	A
4	B	C	A	D
5	A	B	D	C
6	D	A	C	B
7	C	D	B	A
8	B	C	A	D
9	A	B	D	C
10	C	A	B	D
11	C	D	B	A
12	B	C	A	D
Totals				

Parent Observation Profile™ Score Sheet

After making your choices, transfer them onto this chart by circling the letter you chose for each question. Total up each column – each circled letter is worth one point. You should not have a score higher than 12 in any one column. There will be random scores in each column, but there should be one category higher than the others. This is considered a primary personality trait.

	Sunny	Champ	Pal	Max
1	A	B	D	C
2	D	A	C	B
3	C	D	B	A
4	B	C	A	D
5	A	B	D	C
6	D	A	C	B
7	C	D	B	A
8	B	C	A	D
9	A	B	D	C
10	C	A	B	D
11	C	D	B	A
12	B	C	A	D
Totals				

Parent Observation Profile™ Score Sheet

After making your choices, transfer them onto this chart by circling the letter you chose for each question. Total up each column – each circled letter is worth one point. You should not have a score higher than 12 in any one column. There will be random scores in each column, but there should be one category higher than the others. This is considered a primary personality trait.

	Sunny	Champ	Pal	Max
1	A	B	D	C
2	D	A	C	B
3	C	D	B	A
4	B	C	A	D
5	A	B	D	C
6	D	A	C	B
7	C	D	B	A
8	B	C	A	D
9	A	B	D	C
10	C	A	B	D
11	C	D	B	A
12	B	C	A	D
Totals				

Notes

Notes

CPSIA information can be obtained at www.ICGtesting.com
Printed in the USA
BVOW08s2121141214

379310BV00008B/26/P